Homework  3

SOUTHAMPTON
NUMERACY
CENTRE

Mike Askew • Sheila Ebbutt

RIGBY

Homework Response Sheet

Children

What did you like best about this week's homework?

_____

_____

What did you find the easiest thing to do?

_____

_____

What did you find the most difficult thing to do?

_____

_____

Parents

How did your child respond to this week's homework?

_____

_____

Which parts did they find easiest?

_____

_____

Which parts did they find hardest?

_____

_____

Any other comments?

_____

_____

_____

Introduction

The National Numeracy Strategy recommends that mathematics homework should provide a variety of activities that reinforce and extend children's numeracy skills.

This Homework book provides one source of such activities. Numeracy Focus also provides other homework materials through suggestions in the Teaching and Learning File and the Problem of the Week.

These photocopiable Homework pages provide a range of activities:

• work based around the current unit's teaching to consolidate ideas recently introduced

• practice material based on ideas previously covered

• games to consolidate skills and develop strategic thinking

• more open-ended activities to develop using and applying mathematics.

Most of the activities are answered by the children writing directly on to the page. Most pages also contain an activity where more extended recording is required. The children could use the back of the worksheet for this or could use an additional sheet of paper (an icon ☐ is shown if extra paper is needed). Tips and examples are shown in this sort of hint box: ☐

Occasionally an activity requires some counting materials and suggestions are made for items that can be found around the home to use.

Some activities also require dice or number cards – a photocopiable master is provided for both dice and 0–9 cards that you could copy on to card so that each child can have a set to keep at home. The photocopiable master is on page 38.

At the foot of each page there is a brief note to the parent or carer outlining what has been worked on in school that week. In line with the National Numeracy Strategy the activities are presented in ways that do not suggest particular methods of solution. In this way, parents will also be helped to understand the approach to mathematics that is being encouraged.

We suggest that you spend, say, 10 minutes going over the answers with the children when you return the sheets. Marking the homework should provide some diagnostic and formative assessment information. It might be best to go over the homework with the children a couple of days after they have brought it back so that you can concentrate on those activities they found most difficult.

There is also a photocopiable response sheet (opposite) that invites parents and children to comment on the homework. We do not suggest you send this out every week but, say, every half term to encourage parents to become actively involved in their children's work and to contribute to their assessment.

1 Complete.

+10 ▶ 58 ____ 20 ____ 63 ____ 21 ____ 42 ____ 35 ____ 88 ____

+1 ▶ 39 ____ 19 ____ 70 ____ 89 ____ 99 ____ 29 ____ 68 ____

2 Write these numbers in the cross shapes.

Try

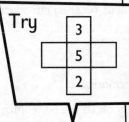

1 2 3 4 5

Make sure each line of three numbers adds up to the same number.

Try doing it three different ways.

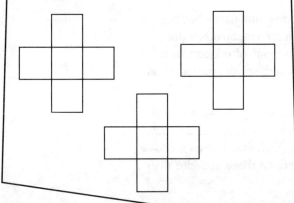

3 Write the missing numbers.

1 102 103 104 _____ 106 107

2 94 95 96 _____ 98 99

3 118 119 _____ 121 122 123

4 67 68 _____ 70 71 72

5 81 82 _____ 84 85 86

6 97 98 99 _____ 101 102

4 ▢ Make 10 in as many ways as you can.

1 + 2 + 3 + 4 = 10
6 + 3 + 1 = 10

You can use any of the digits: 1, 2, 3, 4, 5, 6, 7, 8, 9, and the + sign.

You can use each digit only once in each sum.

5 Write these numbers in order, starting with the biggest.

1 57 75 77 50   ____ ____ ____ ____

2 38 88 83 33 30   ____ ____ ____ ____ ____

3 62 22 60 26 66   ____ ____ ____ ____ ____

4 19 91 109 90 10   ____ ____ ____ ____ ____

● In class your child has begun to learn about numbers to 1000.

1 In each segment of the circle the two outer numbers add to make the inner number.

For example, 6 + 4 = 10.

Fill in the gaps.

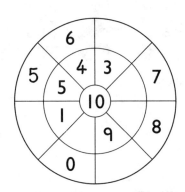
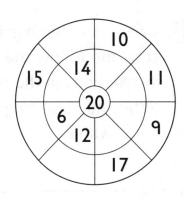

2 Add joining pairs and write the sum in the circle below.

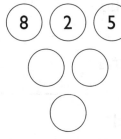
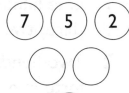

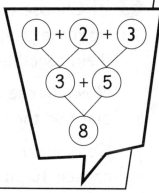

3 Write a number on the mouse.

Write a sum in each segment of the snake that makes the answer on the mouse.

4 Put rings around pairs of numbers in touching boxes that make 20.

5	15	7	13	12	8
15	4	16	7	13	6
12	16	9	5	15	14
8	4	11	9	8	12
10	10	13	11	9	10
9	11	7	13	4	10

5 ▢ Make 20 in as many ways as you can.

You can use any of the digits 2, 3, and 5 and the + sign.

Use each digit as many times as you like.

● *In class your child has been practising adding and subtracting numbers to 20 and beginning to learn some number facts by heart.*

1 Write any number in the star and follow the instructions in the arrows. What number do you finish with?

★ +1 ○ +10 ○ +10 ○ −1 ○
+10 ↓
○ −10 ○ −10 ○ −10 ○

2 📄 Choose two numbers from the stars and add them together.

Now choose another two and add them.

Continue until you have chosen 10 pairs of numbers.

3 Write these numbers in figures.

1 One hundred and thirty two   _____

2 Two hundred and forty one   _____

3 Six hundred and nine   _____

4 Four hundred and thirty three   _____

5 Seven hundred and twenty   _____

6 Ninety nine   _____

4 Join numbers that add to 20.

5	17	6	10	19	16	7	18	9	15
13	4	15	5	3	2	14	1	10	11

● *In class your child has been counting forwards and backwards, and beginning to learn about numbers to 1000.*

1 Someone has spilt paint on these calculations. Can you put them right?

$15 +$ ⬜ 20 ⬜ $- 1 = 17$ ⬜ $+ 5 = 10$

$13 +$ ⬜ 16 ⬜ $- 10 = 20$ $25 + 10 =$ ⬜

$45 -$ ⬜ 44 $39 + 1 =$ ⬜ $20 -$ ⬜ 12

2 Join each shape to its name.

1   cylinder

2   triangular prism

3   hemi-sphere

4   cuboid

5   cube

6   square pyramid

3 Each of the letters in this word is worth the number underneath.

pat
p   a   t
$1 + 3 + 5 = 9$

p	l	a	y	t	i	m	e
1	2	3	4	5	6	7	8

Work out how much each of these words is worth:

1 play _____

2 time _____

3 met _____

4 lay _____

⬜ Make up more words using these letters. What are they worth?

4 ⬜ Use the digits 1, 2, 3, 4 and 5 to make up calculations.

$12 + 3 - 5 + 4 = 14$

Use all the digits every time and use + and – and = .

See if you can make each of the numbers from 1 to 20 as the answers.

● *In class your child has been practising adding and subtracting, and working on 3D shapes.*

1 Look at Tom's work. Mark it and correct the wrong answers.

1 7 + 3 = 10
2 8 + 7 = 14
3 Double 9 = 19
4 12 + 7 = 19
5 2 + 5 + 4 = 10
6 18 − 6 = 13
7 13 + 5 = 16
8 2 + 4 + 3 + 6 = 15

2 You need 15 counters, coins, buttons or pieces of paper.

You can make two different rectangles with 8 buttons.

📄 Record all the different rectangles you can make with 12 buttons.

Now try it with 15 buttons.

3 Work out the answer to each calculation. Each answer stands for a letter.

4 × 2	3 × 4	4 × 6
8	12	24
h	o	t

8	→	h
12	→	o
15	→	y
16	→	w
20	→	d
24	→	t
36	→	u

Find the code words.

1 | 4 × 2 | 4 × 3 | 4 × 4 |

____ ____ ____

2 | 5 × 4 | 2 × 6 |

____ ____

3 | 3 × 5 | 6 × 2 | 6 × 6 |

____ ____ ____

4 | 4 × 5 | 3 × 4 |

____ ____

📄 Make up your own.

4 Complete these multiplication grids.

×	2	3
4	8	
5		

×	4	6
2		
5		

×	2	5
3		
4		

×	5	6
3		
5		

● *In class your child has been learning about multiplication up to 6 times 6.*

1 📄 Make up five multiplications.

Choose one number from each circle for each multiplication.

2   4
3   5

6   4
5   3

2 Write down five things around your home that are about 30 cm long.

1 _____

2 _____

3 _____

4 _____

5 _____

3 Join the name of the object to the nearest approximate length.

bed   10 cm   banana

finger   30 cm   baby's leg

pencil   100 cm   umbrella

walking   2 m   adult
stick

4 Write these lengths in order, starting with the smallest.

1   25 cm   75 cm   15 cm   29 cm   _____ _____ _____ _____

2   32 m   16 m   23 m   61 m   _____ _____ _____ _____

3   2m 10cm   5m 10cm   10m 50cm   2m 5cm   _____ _____ _____ _____

4   105 cm   95 cm   1m 40cm   1m 4cm   _____ _____ _____ _____

● *In class your child has been learning about estimating and measuring length.*

1 In each segment of the circle:

double
half
double

- the inner number is half of the number in the shaded ring
- the outer number is double the number in the shaded ring.

Fill in the spaces.

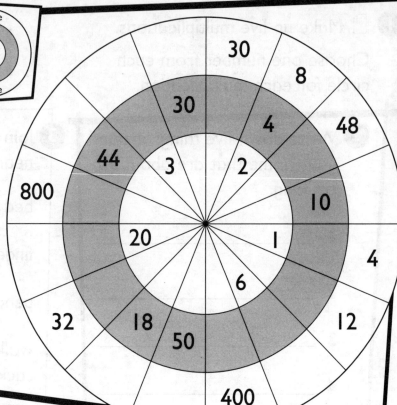

30

8

30

4

48

44

3

2

800

10

20

1

4

6

32

18

12

50

400

2 Look at the crossword clues. Write the answers in words.

Across

1 double five
3 20 – 15
5 halve fourteen
6 6 + 7

Down

1 10 ÷ 5
2 halve eighteen
3 20 – 15
4 double five plus one

3 Draw a ring around each odd number.

2	7	21	13
8	14	3	5
11	4	10	1
9	19	12	6

4 Think of 10 people you know of different ages.

Write down their ages and double each one.

● *In class your child has been working on doubling and halving numbers.*

1 Add 9 to these numbers.

+9 2 ___   7 ___   21 ___   33 ___   28 ___   24 ___

+9 3 ___   15 ___   11 ___   44 ___   10 ___   1 ___

2 Add 11 to the numbers in the top row to find the answer in the bottom row.

(2) 7   21   13   8   14   3   35

32   24   14   25   18   (13)   46   19

3 What's my number?

1 I'm thinking of a number.
   I double it and get 12.
   What's my number?

   _____

2 I'm thinking of a number.
   I take 5 away from it and
   get 15.
   What's my number?

   _____

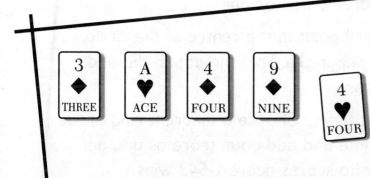

4 *A game for two players.*

You need a pack of playing cards.
Use the Ace to the 10 of both
red suits. Ace counts as one.

Shuffle the cards and share them
out. Take turns to choose a card
and place it face up on the table.

If you can make exactly 21 by
adding your chosen card to some
or all of the cards already on the
table, you win all those cards –
you have won a trick.

Keep each trick separate.

Keep going until you have used
up all the cards.

The winner is the player with
most tricks.

● *In class your child has been learning quick ways of adding 9 and 11.*

1 The box changes the number as it goes through.

Write down what the box does to the number.

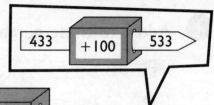

433 → +100 → 533

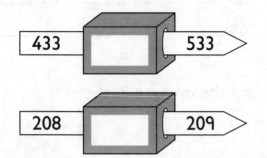

433 → → 533

209 → → 219

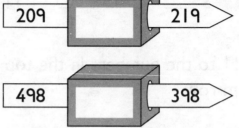

208 → → 209

498 → → 398

2 Join the numbers on the left with the matching sum on the right.

one hundred and forty two	100 + 10 + 5
three hundred and seven	300 + 7
three hundred and seventy	900 + 80 + 2
one hundred and fifteen	100 + 40 + 2
nine hundred and eighty two	300 + 70

3 £1 £1 50p 10p

10p 5p 1p 1p

◻ Make five different amounts using some or all of these coins.

4 *A game for two players.*

◻ You need a paper-clip and a pencil.

Take turns to try to make the target number 543 like this:

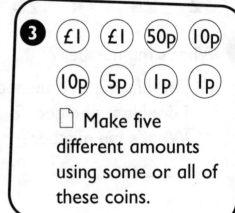

Choose hundreds, tens or ones.

Put your pencil point in the centre of the circle, through the paper-clip. Spin the paper-clip and read your score.

Do this three times. Choose a different ring of the circle each time and add your score as you go. The player who scores nearest 543 wins.

● *In class your child has been practising using three-digit numbers, and adding and subtracting 100, 10 and 1.*

1 Complete.

1 $3 \times 4 = $ ⭐   **2** ⭐ $\times 6 = 12$ **3** ⭐ $\times 7 = 70$

4 $5 \times$ ⭐ $= 15$ **5** $4 \times$ ⭐ $= 24$ **6** ⭐ $\times$ ⭐ $= 25$

2 Write three pairs of numbers that multiply together to make:

1 12 ___3 × 4___ _____ _____

2 16 _____ _____ _____

3 20 _____ _____ _____

3 **1** Mr Baker buys 3 packets of biscuits. There are 6 biscuits in each packet. How many biscuits does Mr Baker buy? _____

2 Sally puts her holiday photos in an album.
Each page of the album holds 4 photos.
Sally has 22 photos. How many pages will she use? _____

4

📄 *A game for two players*

Player 1: Choose a number from the grid (*15*).

Write two numbers which multiply together to give this answer (*3 × 5 = 15*).

9	4	2	15	6	18
10	30	8	16	25	24
3	12	20	5	36	1

Player 2: Check the multiplication. If it is correct, Player 1 crosses out the number (*15*) on the grid.

Player 2 now chooses a number from the grid.

The winner is the first player to cross out three numbers next to each other.

● *In class your child has been working on multiplication and division.*

1 Draw lines joining the numbers with their halves.

8   6   22   18   14   24   10

11   4   7   9   5   12   3

2 You need two dice and some beans, stones or marbles.

Roll the dice and multiply the two numbers.

Collect that number of beans.

If you can divide the number of beans exactly in half, score 1 point.

If you can divide the number of beans exactly into quarters, score 2 points.

What is your score after 10 goes?

3 ▢ *A game for two players*

Before you start:

• Draw a 3 × 3 grid on a piece of paper, big enough to hold a playing card in each box.

• Sort the ace to 9 of clubs from a pack of cards and place them face up on the table.

Take turns to put a card on the grid.

You score a point if you complete a line of 3 cards which add up to an even number. (Diagonals count. The ace counts as one).

Use all the cards and fill the grid. Score two extra points if you place the last card.

Record your game by writing the numbers on a grid.

Play again.

4 Find different ways of colouring in half a square.

● *In class your child has been working on halves, quarters, thirds and fifths.*

1 Add 5 to each number.

45 → ___50___   15 → _____   35 → _____

30 → _____   20 → _____   55 → _____

2 Join the activity to the approximate time it takes.

comb hair	1 second	eat a burger
blink	10 seconds	drink a glass of water
school playtime	1 minute	sneeze
walk 3 kilometres	10 minutes	brush teeth
write your name	1 hour	school dinner break

3 Draw a line to join each time to the correct clock face.

ten past twelve   4:45   six o'clock

quarter to five   6:00   12:10

4 🗋 *A game for two players*

Each player fills their own grid with these numbers: 5, 10, 15, 20, 25, 30, 40, 50, 60.

Take turns to roll a dice. Multiply the number thrown by 5 or 10.

Cross out the answer on your grid. The winner is the first player to cross out all 9 numbers.

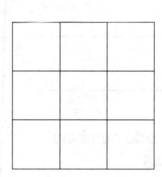

Player 1

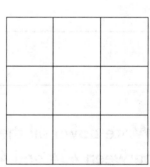

Player 2

● *In class your child has been learning about estimating and measuring time and telling the time.*

1 Write each line of five numbers in order from smallest
to largest and circle the middle number.

1 971   521   151   179   519   _____

2 634   446   368   846   348   _____

3 207   724   470   702   247   _____

2 What number is the arrow
roughly pointing to?

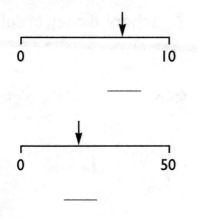

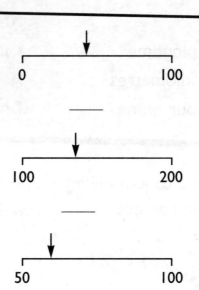

3 Write down all the even numbers
between 213 and 227.

_____

_____

Write down all the odd numbers
between 434 and 448.

_____

_____

4

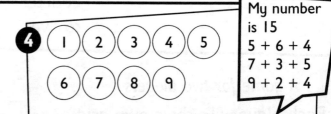

My number
is 15
5 + 6 + 4
7 + 3 + 5
9 + 2 + 4

📄 Choose a number between
11 and 20.
Add up three of the numbers
in the circles to make your
number.

See how many ways you can
make your number with three
circled numbers.

● *In class your child has been learning about numbers to 1000
and odd and even numbers.*

1

| +9 | 18 _____ | 86 _____ | 45 _____ | 27 _____ | 56 _____ |

| +11 | 41 _____ | 19 _____ | 55 _____ | 22 _____ | 35 _____ |

2 Add the numbers in each row and each column.

3	6	7 →	16
9	3	7 →	
1	4	3 →	
13			

2	8	5 →	
5	2	5 →	
5	4	6 →	

4	4	6 →	
7	3	7 →	
6	7	3 →	

3 Split the second number of each sum and use some of it to make the first number a multiple of 10.

26 + 8 ⟶ 26 + 4 + 4 ⟶ 30 + 4

1 37 + 6 _____

2 48 + 7 _____

3 59 + 5 _____

4 66 + 8 _____

5 78 + 8 _____

6 86 + 6 _____

4

1 Choose a number less than 50, for example, 27.

2 Use an empty number line to show how to hop from your number to 100 in exactly 3 hops.

+3   +20   +50

27 hop 1 30 hop 2 50 hop 3 100

3 Do this in five different ways.

• *In class this week your child has been working on adding single digits to two-digit and three-digit numbers.*

1 Pay exactly these amounts using as few coins as you can:

1 44p <u>20p + 20p + 2p + 2p</u>　　2 57p _____

3 66p _____　　4 79p _____

5 34p _____　　6 48p _____

7 93p _____　　8 36p _____

---

2 Zak has £1 to buy three presents. Which three could he buy?

_____

_____

_____

How much change would he get?

_____

joke nose	45p
false moustache	75p
pretend flies	5p
joke soap	35p
ring-through-finger	25p
fake scar	60p
invisible ink	50p
blood capsule	15p

▢ Work out five more combinations of three presents he could afford. Work out the change from £1 each time.

---

3 A vending machine takes only 2p coins. How many coins do you need to pay for each bar of chocolate?

Whizzle   12p ____   Meganut   16p ____

Cruncher 20p ____   Whirlytwirly 18p ____

Another vending machine takes only 5p coins. How many coins do you need to pay for these drinks?

Frisssh   35p ____   Poptastic   50p ____

Guzzler   25p ____   Slurpz   40p ____

4 ▢ Invisible ink costs 50p.

Can you pay for it exactly with:

1 coin?

2 coins?

3 coins?

4 coins?

Show clearly how you worked out the answers.

● *In class your child has been learning about adding and subtracting with money.*

1 Fill in the missing numbers to make the scales balance.

30	8		38

40	5		

47			53

25			30

38	7		

69			76

2 Join the item to the nearest approximate weight.

mouse	10 grams	cup
pencil	100 grams	kettle of water
dog	1 kilogram	banana
apple	10 kilograms	bucket of water

3 Double each number.

32	→	64
25	→	
16	→	
55	→	
400	→	

4 Who is heavier?

1 Petra or Max?

_____

2 Sadika or Petra?

_____

3 Petra or Jess?

_____

4 Sadika or Jess?

_____

5 Max or Sadika?

_____

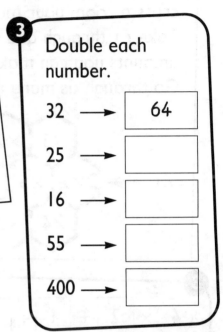

5 Draw arrows joining pairs of numbers to show 'is heavier than'.

There are 6 arrows for each box

442g
344g
400g
404g

766g
677g
676g
777g

● *In class your child has been estimating and measuring weight.*

1 Draw a line joining each number with its double.

44	34	21	18	25	31	24	20
42	62	40	48	88	50	36	68

2 🗎 These are magic rooms. When you cross a room your money multiplies. Take £1 through and see what different amounts you can make.
Go through as many rooms as you like.

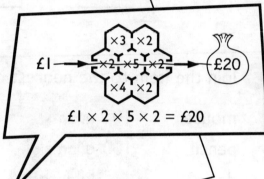

£1 × 2 × 5 × 2 = £20

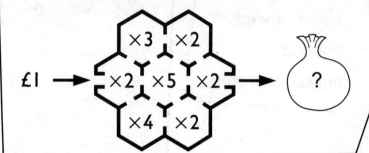

3

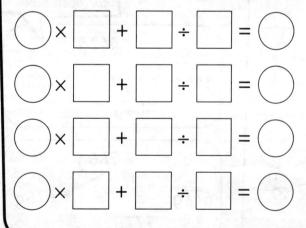

Roll a dice twice. Put one of the numbers in the first circle and the other in the last circle. Put any other numbers in the boxes to make the number sentence work.

○ × ☐ + ☐ ÷ ☐ = ○

○ × ☐ + ☐ ÷ ☐ = ○

○ × ☐ + ☐ ÷ ☐ = ○

○ × ☐ + ☐ ÷ ☐ = ○

4 You need coins.

🗎 Draw two circles and put coins in them.

• The second circle must have twice as many coins as the first.

• The coins in the two circles must add up to the same amount.

Draw your answers.
Find as many different ways as you can.

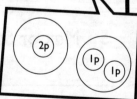

● *In class your child has been learning about multiplying and dividing.*

1 Write a number that is between the other two numbers.

200 _____ 250   300 _____ 340   450 _____ 460

195 _____ 205   564 _____ 568   333 _____ 335

2 Draw a pattern on each shape to make a shape with two lines of symmetry.

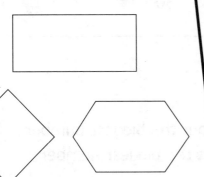

3 ▢ Carefully copy or trace these shapes and cut them out. Put them together to make symmetrical shapes. Draw your symmetrical shapes. How many can you find?

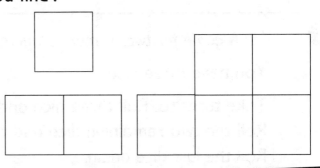

4 Shade the fraction shown on each shape.

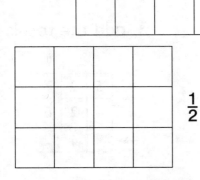

$\frac{1}{3}$

$\frac{1}{2}$

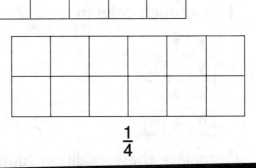

$\frac{1}{4}$

5 Write down the difference between each pair of numbers.

402, 398 ⟶ 4   39, 43 ⟶   268, 271 ⟶   142, 137 ⟶

201, 199 ⟶   448, 452 ⟶   93, 87 ⟶   506, 503 ⟶

● *In class your child has been working on symmetry.*

❶ Complete.

	23	42	56	68	33	20	62	11	34	55	47	19
add 10	33											
add 20		62										
add 30			86									

❷ Join pairs of numbers that add up to 100.

25 20 15 55 40 30 65 50 10 75 70 45

35 25 60 75 55 90 45 50 80 70 85 30

❸ 🗋 *A game for two or more players.*

You need three dice.

Take turns to: Roll three dice and take out the biggest number.
Roll the two remaining dice and take out the biggest number.
Roll the last dice again.

Add up the numbers on all three dice – that is your score. Add up
your score over several rounds. The first person to score 100 wins.

❹ For each addition square:

1 add each column

5	2	
4	2	
9	4	

2 add each row

5	2	7
4	2	6
9	4	

3 add the totals

5	2	7
4	2	6
9	4	13

Complete these addition squares.

8	4	
6	9	

5		11
	7	
8		

6		8
	11	20

7		

		20

● *In class your child has been adding and subtracting two-digit numbers.*

1 Count on in threes:

_6_ _9_ _12_ ___ ___ ___ ___ ___ ___ ___

Count on in fours:

_3_ _7_ _11_ ___ ___ ___ ___ ___ ___ ___

Count on in fives:

_1_ _6_ _11_ ___ ___ ___ ___ ___ ___ ___

2 Loop the pairs of near doubles that are next to each other.

22	17	18	65	67
23	24	16	17	66
71	14	15	40	68
70	15	38	39	50
69	27	28	29	51

Use doubling to add near doubles.

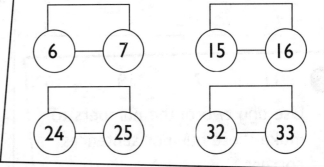

3 Add the numbers on the wheels. Write the answer in the truck.

4 Fill in the wheels with near doubles. The wheels must add up to the number in the truck.

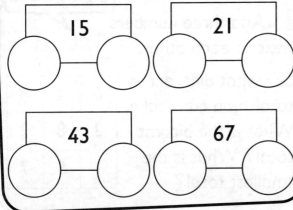

5 Make up 4 wheel and truck problems.

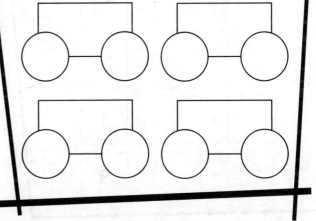

● In class your child has been working on using doubles and near doubles.

1 Join each number to its double.

(25)   45   80   55   65   90   35   75

160   130   70   (50)   150   90   180   110

2 Write each number in the correct area of the Venn diagram below.

5 7 20 12 15 10 18
8 30 24 6 36 25 11

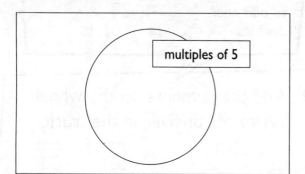

multiples of 5

3 You need two dice.

Roll two dice and add up the score. Colour in a square on the graph above that number.

Roll the dice again and add up the score. Keep doing this until one of the lines is full.

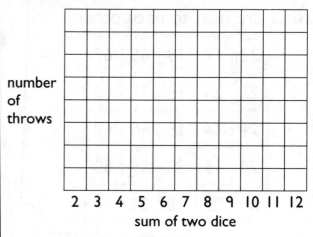

number of throws

2 3 4 5 6 7 8 9 10 11 12
sum of two dice

Which scores did you get least of? _____

4   11   7   19   16

Use any two of the numbers to make these number sentences correct.

☐ + ☐ = 26

☐ + ☐ = 30

☐ + ☐ = 23

☐ + ☐ = 3

☐ + ☐ = 9

5 ☐ Add three numbers next to each other.

6 + 4 + 8 = 18

See what different totals you can make. What is the biggest total? What is the smallest total?

6	4	9
3	8	2
1	5	7

● *In class your child has been learning about graphs and charts.*

1 Divide each number by 3.   15 —— 24 —— 30 —— 21 —— 60 ——

        Divide each number by 5.   15 —— 25 —— 40 —— 100 —— 60 ——

---

2 Join each sentence to the correct number sentence.

Share fifty among five

Share ten among five

Ten divided by five

$50 \div 5$

$10 \div 5$

$50 \div 10$

How many groups of ten are there in fifty?

Divide fifty by five

---

3 📄 *A game for two players.*

You need some dried beans, buttons, counters or pieces of paper.

Each player grabs some beans. Put the beans into groups. Score like this:

Groups of 2 with no remainder → 1 point
Groups of 3 with no remainder → 2 points
Groups of 4 with no remainder → 4 points

If you can divide the beans in more than one way, add each score. Play 5 rounds. The player with most points wins.

4 Mr Chick collects 22 eggs. Each egg box holds 6 eggs. How many egg boxes does Mr Chick need to hold all his eggs?

_____

---

5 The numbers on the wheels add to make the number on the truck. Fill in the numbers on the wheels.

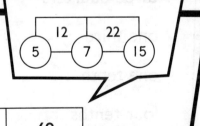

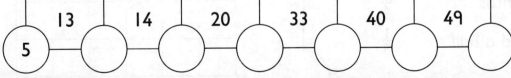

• *In class your child has been working on division.*

1 The number 3 in the middle diamond starts all the calculations.

Fill in the missing answers in the circles and the missing calculations in the boxes to make eight multiplication statements.

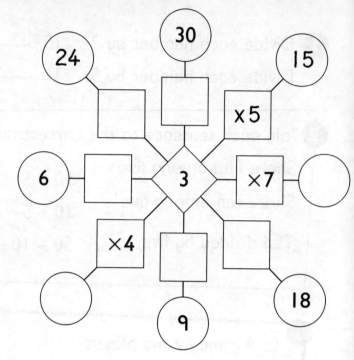

2 Finish shading in these diagrams to show the correct fraction.

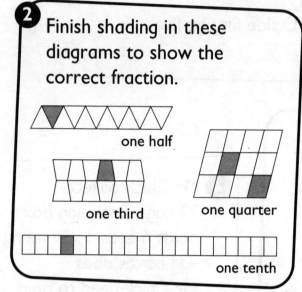

one half

one third

one quarter

one tenth

3 You need three colouring pencils: one red, one blue and one green.

Follow these rules to make a pattern on the grid below.

• Half of the squares must be red.

• One third of the squares must be green.

• The rest of the squares must be blue.

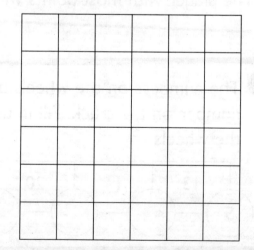

4 Draw lines to join the words to the matching fractions.

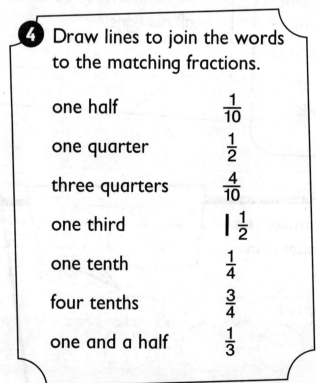

one half $\frac{1}{10}$

one quarter $\frac{1}{2}$

three quarters $\frac{4}{10}$

one third $1\frac{1}{2}$

one tenth $\frac{1}{4}$

four tenths $\frac{3}{4}$

one and a half $\frac{1}{3}$

• *In class your child has been learning about fractions.*

1 Halve each number.

16 _____   24 _____   30 _____   40 _____   50 _____   100 _____

Find a quarter of each number.

12 _____   24 _____   40 _____   100 _____   60 _____   300 _____

2 How many of each of these shapes can you find in the picture?

square   _____

triangle   _____

hexagon   _____

octagon   _____

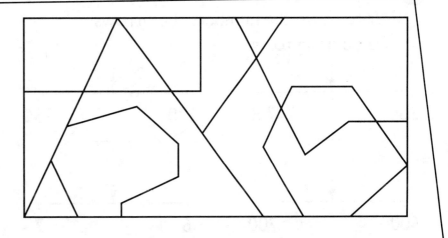

3 Shade each strip to show a half. Make each pattern different.

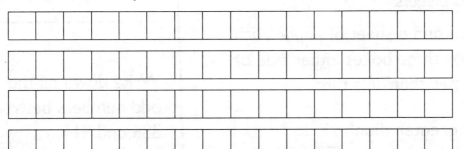

4 The numbers on the wheels add to the number on the truck. Fill in the missing numbers.

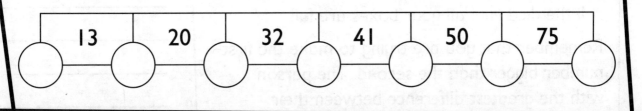

Numeracy Focus 3: Homework

25

• In class your child has been working on 2D shapes.

1 📄 Write each line of four prices in order from smallest to largest.

1 £8.52 £5.28 £1.82 £8.25 _____

2 £6.38 £8.36 £4.68 £8.04 _____

3 £6.99 £9.66 £6.09 £9.16 _____

2 The arrow points to the middle number.
Write down the numbers the arrows
are pointing to.

3 Write down all the even numbers between 579 and 607.

_____

_____

_____

_____

_____

_____

_____

```
        ↓                      ↓
  |_____|          |_____|
500          700        220         230
     _____                    _____

        ↓                      ↓
  |_____|          |_____|
600          700        6           7
     _____                    _____
```

4 📄 *A game for two players.*

You need one dice and a sheet of paper each.
Each person draws three boxes either side of
the words 'is greater than' like this:

```
┌──┬──┬──┐                 ┌──┬──┬──┐
│  │  │  │  'is greater than'  │  │  │  │
└──┴──┴──┘                 └──┴──┴──┘
```

Player 1 rolls the dice. Both players secretly
write the number in one of their boxes.

Player 2 rolls the dice. Both players write the
number in another of their boxes. Continue to
roll the dice until all your boxes are full.

Remember that you are trying to make the first
number bigger than the second. The person
with the greatest difference between their
numbers wins.

Write down all the
odd numbers between
886 and 914.

_____

_____

_____

_____

_____

_____

_____

● *In class your child has been learning about numbers to 1000.*

1 Fill in the missing numbers to make the scales balance.

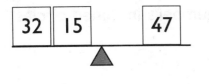
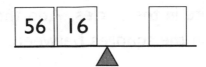
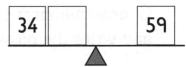

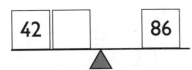

2 Draw arrows joining pairs of numbers to show 'is greater than'.

There are 6 arrows for each box

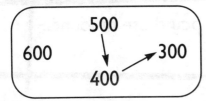
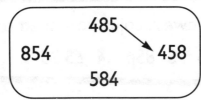
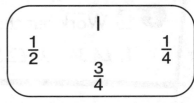

3 Raj has 21 stamps in one album and 39 stamps in another album. He gives away 25 stamps. How many stamps does Raj have left? _____

Dan bakes 4 trays of cakes. Each tray holds 10 cakes. When the cakes are cool, Dan puts the cakes into bags. He puts 5 cakes in each bag. How many bags does Dan need?

_____

5 Make each number up to 100.

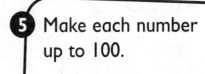

$55 +$ ⟶ 100

$35 +$ ⟶ 100

$75 +$ ⟶ 100

$60 +$ ⟶ 100

4 ▢ Choose one number from each row.
Add them together.
Make exactly 100 in as many ways as you can.

10	20	30
20	30	40
40	50	60

● In class your child has been working on adding and subtracting two-digit numbers.

1   17   19   23   36   42   28   35   15   9   11

Choose numbers to write in the circles. Add the numbers in joined circles and write the answers in the squares between.

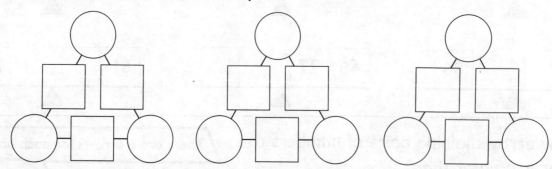

2 📄 Work out the fewest coins you need to pay these amounts:

1 £4.34   **2** £2.56   **3** 85p   **4** £5.25

3 To draw this line you start at A1, and then you go: A2, B2, B3, D3, D4, D5, E5.

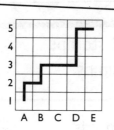

Draw your own line from A1 to E5.

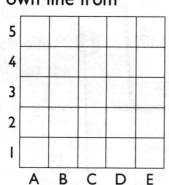

📄 Write the instructions for drawing it.

Give the instructions to someone else and see whether they can draw your line.

4 Complete this crossword puzzle. Write the answers in words.

Across	Down
1 71 – 58	**1** 90 ÷ 9
3 Half of 38	**2** 98 – 87
5 72 – 70 + 1	**4** The opposite
6 800 – 799	of odd
	5 10 ÷ 5

● *In class your child has been learning about coordinates.*

1 Fill in the table.

	× 2	× 5	× 10
3	6	15	30
5			
7			
4			
8			
6			
2			
9			

2 Draw a circle around each number that can be divided by 2 exactly.

125   10   345

122

999

12

534   354

998

15   221

3 Complete the multiplications.

$3 \times 5 \rightarrow$ [15] $\times 2 \rightarrow$ [30]   [3] $\times 10 \rightarrow$ [30]

$2 \times 5 \rightarrow$ [ ] $\times 2 \rightarrow$ [ ]   [ ] $\times 10 \rightarrow$ [ ]

$6 \times 5 \rightarrow$ [ ] $\times 2 \rightarrow$ [ ]   [ ] $\times 10 \rightarrow$ [ ]

$5 \times 5 \rightarrow$ [ ] $\times 2 \rightarrow$ [ ]   [ ] $\times 10 \rightarrow$ [ ]

$4 \times 5 \rightarrow$ [ ] $\times 2 \rightarrow$ [ ]   [ ] $\times 10 \rightarrow$ [ ]

$7 \times 5 \rightarrow$ [ ] $\times 2 \rightarrow$ [ ]   [ ] $\times 10 \rightarrow$ [ ]

4 Geeta secretly thought of two numbers. When she added her numbers she got 7. When she multiplied her numbers together she got 10.

What were her two numbers? _____ _____

Make up two more secret puzzles like this.

● *In class your child has been working on multiples of 2, 5 and 10.*

1 Complete.

	23	42	56	68	33	20	62	11	34	55	47	19
add 9												
add 19												
add 29												

2 📄 Write down pairs of numbers that add up to 1000.

250	200	150	550	400	300	250	850
350	500	400	50	200	900	450	150
100	750	700	450	650	550	600	800
800	600	590	680	500	850	950	750

3 Use any two of these numbers to make the calculations correct.

6	6	3	4	4	5	5	10

$$\square \times \square = 18 \qquad 30 \div \square = \square$$

$$\square \times \square = 15 \qquad 36 \div \square = \square$$

$$\square \times \square = 24 \qquad 50 \div \square = \square$$

$$\square \times \square = 12 \qquad 25 \div \square = \square$$

$$\square \times \square = 40 \qquad 16 \div \square = \square$$

4

> man
> m a n
> $8 + 7 + 1 = 16$

Each of the letters in this word is worth the number underneath.

n o i s y   c a m e l
1 2 3 4 5   6 7 8 9 10

Work out how much each of these words is worth:

1 lemon _____

2 lime _____

3 money _____

4 coin _____

5 📄 Use the numbers 2, 5 and 6. Use × or + or both. Make the following:

1 The largest even number.　　**2** A multiple of 10.

3 The smallest even number.　　**4** A number over 30.

5 A number which is double another number.

● *In class your child has been learning about multiplication and division.*

1 Continue the number patterns.

1 9, 12, ☐ , ☐ , ☐ , ☐ , 27, ☐ , ☐ , 36, 39

2 36, ☐ , 44, 48, ☐ , ☐ , 60, ☐ , 68, ☐ , 76

3 ☐ , 40, 48, ☐ , 64, ☐ , 80, ☐ , ☐ , 104, 112

2 Write the numbers in the correct places.

Add five more numbers and write them in their places.

8   10
50
25
32
30   45
100
102   105

multiples of 5	not multiples of 5
15	6

3 Write 'is less than' or 'is greater than' between the numbers.

48   50

149   124

200   100

399   400

925   915

2          $1\frac{1}{2}$

4 ☐ Mark was born on 7 March 1989, Mark's birthday can be written 7/3/89.

Using the digits in his birthday 7, 3, 8, 9 Mark can write calculations to make different numbers.

$7 + 3 + 8 + 9 = 27$
$3 \times 7 + 89 = 110$

When is your birthday? Write the digits in your birth date. What numbers can you make from the digits?

● In class your child has been working on numbers and handling data.

1 The box changes the number as it goes through.
Write down what the box does to the number.

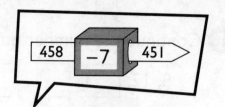

458 → −7 → 451

603 → → 597

209 → → 199

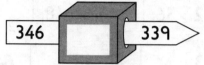

346 → → 339

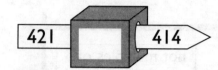

421 → → 414

389 → → 381

105 → → 97

2 Add 31 to the numbers on the top row and find the answer.

(10)   47   21   63   28   54   33   11

59   94   78   85   42   (41)   64   52

3

1 I'm thinking of a number.
   I double it and get 120.
   What's my number? _____

2 I'm thinking of a number.
   I add 300 to it and get 700.
   What's my number? _____

3 I'm thinking of a number.
   I halve it and get 450.
   What's my number? _____

4 I'm thinking of a number.
   I take away 33 from it and get
   45. What's my number? _____

4 Oh no! Someone has spilt paint on the
calculations! Can you put them right?

651 + ⬤ = 660

398 + ⬤ = 400

138 + ⬤ = 140

725 + ⬤ = 730

453 − ⬤ = 450

357 + 3 = ⬤

⬤ − 1 = 240

200 − ⬤ = 195

5

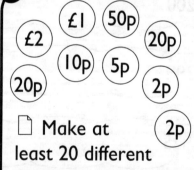

£2   £1   50p   20p
20p   10p   5p
20p   2p
2p

☐ Make at
least 20 different
amounts using
some of these coins.

● *In class your child has been learning about addition and subtraction.*

1 Multiply each number by 2.

7 _____   13 _____   6 _____

9 _____   11 _____   20 _____

Multiply each number by 5.

10 _____   4 _____   7 _____

6 _____   9 _____   20 _____

2 📄 Multiply pairs of numbers next to each other to make 12 calculations.

2	3	6
6	4	10
5	6	3

3

1 Write down the number in the circle that is not in the hexagon or the pentagon. _____

2 Write down the numbers that are in both the hexagon and pentagon. _____

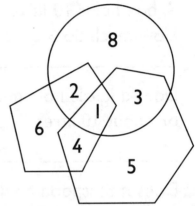

3 Write down the number that is in the circle and the hexagon and the pentagon. _____

4 Fill in the missing numbers. Multiply the two numbers next to the multiplication sign and put the number in the square above.

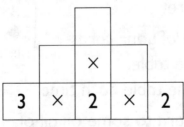

	10	
2	×	5

4	×	2
2	×	2	×	1

	×	
3	×	2	×	2

	×	
5	×	2	×	2

5 Meg was five years old when her baby brother was born. How old will she be when she is twice as old as her brother? _____

● *In class your child has been working on memorizing multiplication and division facts.*

1 📄 Choose a number from the first circle.

Choose a calculation from the second circle.
Work out the answer. Make up 10.

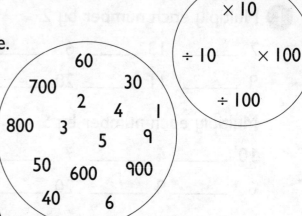

2 1 How many millilitres
are there in a litre? _____

2 A box holds 10 litres.
How much do 6 boxes hold?
_____

3 Does a kettle hold about 1 litre
or about 10 litres? _____
_____

4 Does a teaspoon hold about 5 ml
or about 500 ml? _____

3 📄 Find containers at
home that hold
these amounts.
Write down the
containers' names.

1 About 50 ml
2 About 100 ml
3 About 250 ml
4 About 500 ml
5 About 750 ml
6 About 1 litre

4 *A game for two players*

You need a pack of playing cards.
Use all the cards from both red suits.

Ace = 1   Jack = 11
Queen = 12   King = 13.

Shuffle the cards. Share them all out.
Look at your cards in secret.

Take turns to choose one of your cards
and place it face up on the table.
Add up all the cards on the table each time.

If you can add your last card to some or all of
the cards on the table to make 30, you win all those
cards – you have won a trick. Keep going until you
have used up all the cards. The winner is the player
with most tricks.

● *In class your child has been learning about capacity, and about solving problems.*

1 Draw lines to join the pairs that are the same amount.

Five pounds and sixty pence	£6.50
Six pounds and fifty pence	£5.06
Five pounds and six pence	£5.60

2 Shade the fractions.

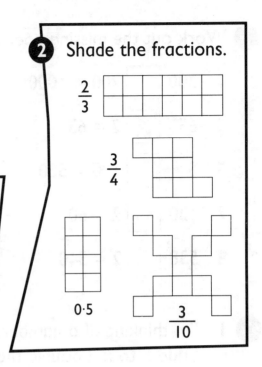

$\frac{2}{3}$

$\frac{3}{4}$

0·5

$\frac{3}{10}$

3 Use these 9 numbers and + or − to make up three addition or subtraction sentences.

34 58 60 67 76 85 110 125 145

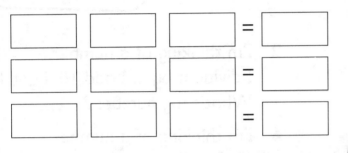

4 There are four calculations in this diagram, three across and one down.

Use the numbers 1 to 9. Put a different number in each box.

Each calculation must be correct.

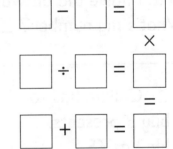

5 How many circles are there? DO NOT COUNT THEM ALL. Look for a pattern. _____

● *In class your child has been working on adding three-digit and two-digit numbers.*

1 Work out the missing operation + − × or ÷ .

1 300 ☐ 700 = 1000   2 33 ☐ 44 = 77

3 65 ☐ 2 = 63   4 52 ☐ 9 = 61

5 5 ☐ 100 = 500   6 60 ☐ 10 = 6

7 120 ☐ 2 = 60   8 700 ☐ 2 = 350

9 538 ☐ 2 = 540   10 357 ☐ 7 = 350

2 ▢ Choose five of the calculations from question 1.

Write a story to go with each calculation.

3 1 I'm thinking of a number. I add 5 to it. I double the answer. I get 18. What's my number? ____

2 I'm thinking of a number. I divide it by 5. I add 10. I get 13. What's my number? ____

3 I'm thinking of a number. I add 6 to it, I halve the answer. I get 9. What's my number? ____

4 I'm thinking of a number. I subtract 4 from it. I multiply by 3. I get 12. What's my number? ____

4 ▢ Callum has to buy 3 presents. He has £5.

Work out six different choices Callum has.

Work out the change from £5 each time.

£2.60 £1.15 £1.20 £3.55 £2.45 50p £2.05 95p

HITS OF THE 90's

● *In class your child has been learning about addition and subtraction.*

1 🖹 Add pairs of numbers next to each other to make 12 calculations from this grid.

40	55	30
60	25	50
30	25	45

2 Put a cross next to all the right-angles that you can find in this diagram.

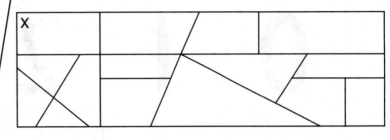

x

3 On this diagram, any straight line of 3 circles adds up to the same total.

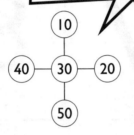

40 + 30 + 20 = 90
10 + 30 + 50 = 90

Fill in the circles on the diagram below with these numbers:

| 10 20 30 40 50 60 70 |

Each straight line of 3 circles should add up to the same total.

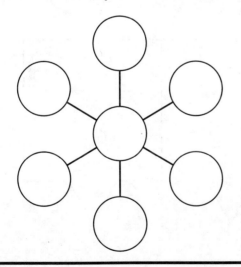

4 Draw a line joining each angle to the correct description.

1

2

3

4

5

6

7

8

greater than a right-angle

a right-angle

less than a right-angle

5 Can you cut a round cake into 8 pieces with only 3 cuts?

(You cannot cut the cake in layers.)

_____

● *In class your child has been working on angles.*

37

0–9 cards

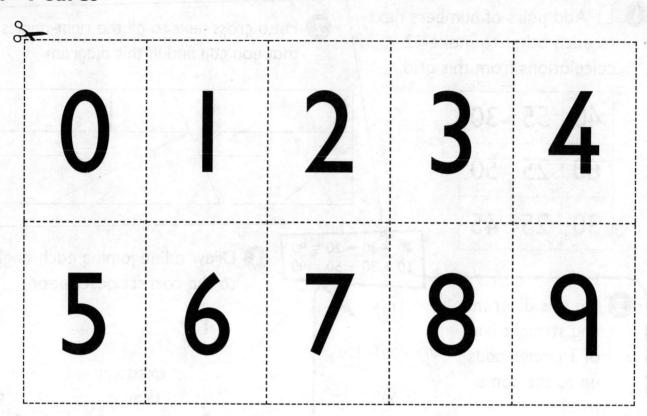

Dice

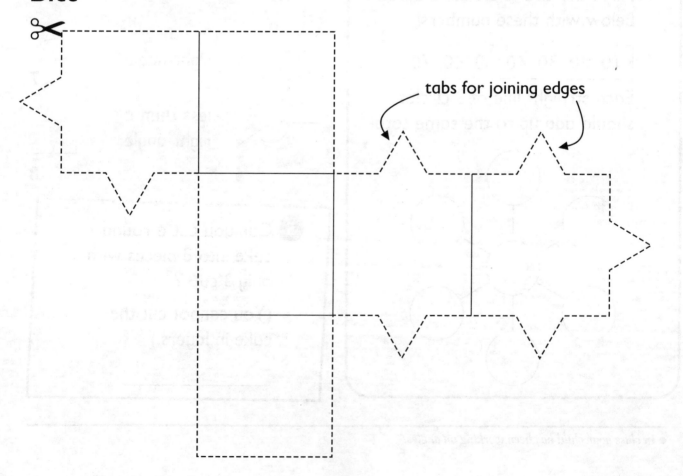

tabs for joining edges